GUITAR • VOCAL

STRUM & SING

Yesterday

MUSIC FROM THE ORIGINAL MOTION PICTURE SOUNDTRACK

© 2019 UNIVERSAL STUDIOS

ISBN 978-1-5400-6432-5

HAL•LEONARD®

Visit Hal Leonard Online at
www.halleonard.com

Contact us:
Hal Leonard
7777 West Bluemound Road
Milwaukee, WI 53213
Email: info@halleonard.com

In Europe, contact:
Hal Leonard Europe Limited
42 Wigmore Street
Marylebone, London, W1U 2RN
Email: info@halleonardeurope.com

In Australia, contact:
Hal Leonard Australia Pty. Ltd.
4 Lentara Court
Cheltenham, Victoria, 3192 Australia
Email: info@halleonard.com.au

All You Need Is Love

Words and Music by
John Lennon and Paul McCartney

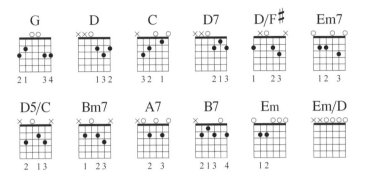

Intro

|G   D |G |C   D7 |

|G   D/F♯ |Em7 |
Love, love,   love,

|G   D/F♯ |Em7 |
Love, love,   love,

|D7   G |D7 |
Love, love,   love.

|D   D5/C |Bm7 D ||

Verse 1

|G   D/F♯ |Em7 |
   There's nothing you can do that can't be done,

|G   D/F♯ |Em7 |
   Nothing you can sing that can't be sung,

|D7   G |
   Nothing you can say,

|D   D7 |
But you can learn how to play the game,

|D   D5/C |Bm7 D ||
It's easy.

Verse 2

```
|G                 D/F♯              |Em7      |
   Nothing you can make that can't be made,
|G       D/F♯           |Em7            |
   No one you can save that can't be saved,
|D7              G
   Nothing you can do,
                  |D                  D7
But you can learn how to be you in time,
      |D   D5/C |Bm7  D        ||
It's easy.
```

Chorus 1

```
|G      A7  |D    D7      |
   All you need is love,
|G      A7  |D    D7      |
   All you need is love,
|G        B7  |Em  Em/D    |
   All you need is love, love,
|C        D7           |G        ||
   Love is all you need.
```

Solo

```
|G     D/F♯|Em7       |
(Love, love,  love.)
|G     D/F♯|Em7       |
(Love, love,  love.)
|D7   G    |D  D7     |
(Love, love,  love.)
|D   D5/C |Bm7  D      ||
```

Chorus 2

```
|G      A7   |D    D7   |
  All you need is love,
|G      A7   |D    D7   |
  All you need is love,
|G      B7   |Em  Em/D  |
  All you need is love, love,
|C      D7        |G     ‖
  Love is all you need.
```

Verse 3

```
|G              D/F♯            |Em7    |
  There's nothing you can know that isn't known,
|G              D/F♯       |Em7       |
  There's nothing you can see that isn't shown,
|D7                  G
  There's nowhere you can be
          |D              D7
That isn't where you're meant to be,
    |D  D5/C |Bm7  D        ‖
It's easy.
```

Chorus 3   *Repeat Chorus 2*

Chorus 4   *Repeat Chorus 2*

Outro

```
|G          |
  Love is all  you need. (Love is all you need.)
           |                           |
Love is all  you need. (Love is all you need.)
‖:          |
  Love is all  you need. (Love is all you need.)
           |                        :‖ Repeat and fade
Love is all  you need. (Love is all you need.)
```

Carry That Weight

Words and Music by
John Lennon and Paul McCartney

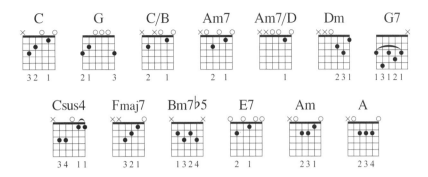

Chorus 1

$\quad$ **C** $\qquad$ |**G** $\qquad$ |
Boy, you're gonna carry that weight,
$\qquad\qquad$ |**C** $\qquad$ |
Carry that weight a long time.
$\qquad$ |**G** $\qquad$ |
Boy, you're gonna carry that weight,
$\qquad\qquad$ |**C** $\qquad$ **C/B** ||
Carry that weight a long time.

Interlude

|**Am7** $\qquad$ |**Am7/D Dm** |**G7** $\qquad$ |**Csus4 C** $\qquad$ |
|**Fmaj7** $\qquad$ |**Bm7♭5 E7** |**Am** $\qquad$ ||

Verse

Am7 $\qquad\qquad$ |**Am7/D Dm** |**G7**
$\quad$ I never give you my pil $\quad$ - $\quad$ low,
$\qquad\qquad$ |**Csus4 C** $\qquad$ |**Fmaj7**
I only send you my invi $\quad$ - $\quad$ tations,
$\qquad\qquad$ |**Bm7♭5 E7** $\qquad$ |**Am7** $\qquad$ **G** | **C** $\quad$ **G**|
And in the middle of the cele $\quad$ - $\quad$ brations I break down.

Chorus 2

$\quad$ **C** $\qquad$ |**G** $\qquad$ |
Boy, you're gonna carry that weight,
$\qquad\qquad$ |**C** $\qquad$ |
Carry that weight a long time.
$\qquad$ |**G** $\qquad$ |
Boy, you're gonna carry that weight,
$\qquad\qquad$ |**C** $\qquad$ **C/B** |**A** $\qquad$ |
Carry that weight a long time.
|**C** $\qquad$ **C/B** |**A** $\qquad$ ||

Back in the U.S.S.R.

Words and Music by
John Lennon and Paul McCartney

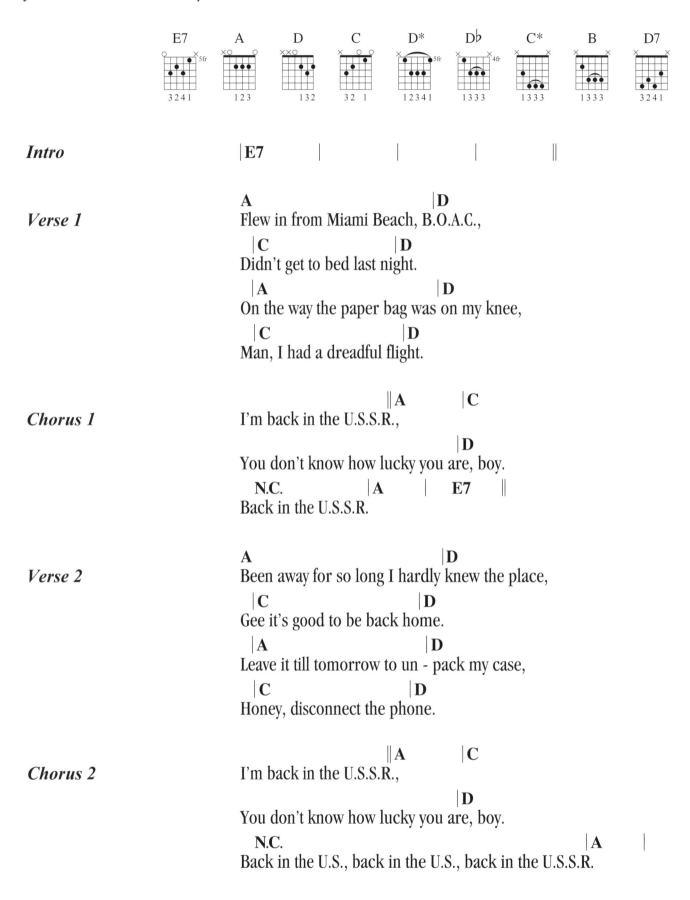

Intro

|E7 | | | ||

Verse 1

A |D
Flew in from Miami Beach, B.O.A.C.,
|C |D
Didn't get to bed last night.
|A |D
On the way the paper bag was on my knee,
|C |D
Man, I had a dreadful flight.

Chorus 1

||A |C
I'm back in the U.S.S.R.,
|D
You don't know how lucky you are, boy.
N.C. |A | E7 ||
Back in the U.S.S.R.

Verse 2

A |D
Been away for so long I hardly knew the place,
|C |D
Gee it's good to be back home.
|A |D
Leave it till tomorrow to un - pack my case,
|C |D
Honey, disconnect the phone.

Chorus 2

||A |C
I'm back in the U.S.S.R.,
|D
You don't know how lucky you are, boy.
N.C. |A |
Back in the U.S., back in the U.S., back in the U.S.S.R.

Bridge 1

```
                    ‖ D            |
Well, the Ukraine girls really knock me out,
         | A                  |
They leave the West behind,
         | D*      Db        | C*        B
And Moscow girls make me sing and shout
         | E7                    | D7             | A     |   E7    ‖
That Georgia's always on my mi-mi-mi-mi-mi-mi-mi-mind.
```

Solo

```
| A        D |        | C        D |        A |
|          D |        | C
```

Chorus 3

```
D |                        ‖ A        | C
Hey, I'm back in the U.S.S.R.,
                                    | D
You don't know how lucky you are, boys,
  N.C.              | A        |
Back in the U.S.S.R.
```

Bridge 2

```
                    ‖ D            |
Well, the Ukraine girls really knock me out,
         | A                  |
They leave the West behind,
         | D*      Db        | C*        B
And Moscow girls make me sing and shout
         | E7                    | D7             | A     |   E7
That Georgia's always on my mi-mi-mi-mi-mi-mi-mi-mind.    Oh. ___
```

Verse 3

```
          ‖ A                              | D
Show me 'round your snow-peaked mountains way down south,
  | C                    | D
Take me to your daddy's farm.
  | A                    | D
Let me hear your balalaikas ringing out,
  | C                        | D
Come and keep your comrade warm.
```

Chorus 4

```
                    ‖ A        | C
I'm back in the U.S.S.R.,
                            | D
You don't know how lucky you are, boy.
  N.C.              | A
Back in the U.S.S.R.
  |        E7            ‖
Oh, let me tell you, honey.
```

Outro

```
‖: A        |                :‖ Play 3 times
```

A Hard Day's Night

Words and Music by
John Lennon and Paul McCartney

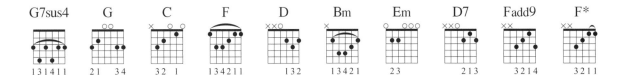

Verse 1

|G7sus4 |G   C |G
   It's been a hard day's night,
             |F |G
And I've been working like a dog.
      | C |G
It's been a hard day's night,
           |F |G
I should be sleeping like a log.
          |C
But when I get home to you,
           |D
I find the things that you do,
         |G   C |G
Will make me feel al - right.

Verse 2

         ‖G   C |G
You know I work all day,
         |F |G
To get you money to buy you things.
        | C |G
And it's worth it just to hear you say,
          |F |G
You're gonna give me ev'ry - thing.
         |C
So why on earth should I moan,
         |D
'Cause when I get you alone,
       |G   C |G
You know I feel O.   K.

Bridge 1

‖ **Bm** |
When I'm home

| **Em** | **Bm** |
 Ev'rything seems to be right.

| | **G** |
  When I'm home,

| **Em** |
 Feeling you holding me

| **C** | **D7** ‖
 Tight, tight, yeah.

Verse 3 *Repeat Verse 1*

Solo ‖: **G C** | **G** | **F** | **G** :‖ **G**

[1.] ⌐────⌐ [2.]

Verse 4

‖ **C**
 So why on earth should I moan,

 | **D**
'Cause when I get you alone,

 | **G C** | **G**
You know I feel O. K.

Bridge 2 *Repeat Bridge 1*

Verse 5 *Repeat Verse 1*

Outro

C ‖ **G C** | **G**
 You know I feel al - right,

C | **G C** | **Fadd9 F*** ‖
 You know I feel al - right.

‖: **Fadd9 F*** | **Fadd9 F*** :‖ *Repeat and fade*

Help!

Words and Music by
John Lennon and Paul McCartney

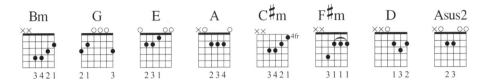

Intro

Bm | |
(Help!) I need somebody.
G | |
(Help!) Not just anybody.
E | |
(Help!) You know I need someone.
A | ‖
(Help!)

Verse 1

A | |C#m | |F#m
　When I was younger, so much younger than to - day,
| |D G |A |
I never needed anybody's help in any way.
| |C#m | |F#m
But now those days are gone and I'm not so self-as - sured,
| |D G |A ‖
Now I find I've changed my mind, and opened up the doors.

Chorus 1

Bm | | |
Help me if you can, I'm feeling down,
    |**G** | | | |
And I do appreciate you being 'round.
E | |
Help me get my feet back on the ground.
    |**A** | | | ‖
Won't you please, please help me?

Verse 2

A | |**C♯m** | |**F♯m**
  And now my life has changed in oh, so many ways.
    | |**D** **G** |**A** |
My inde - pendence seems to vanish in the haze.
    | |**C♯m** | |**F♯m**
But ev'ry now and then I feel so inse - cure.
    | |**D** **G** |**A**
I know that I just need you like I've never done before.

Chorus 2   *Repeat Chorus 1*

Verse 3   *Repeat Verse 1*

Chorus 3

Bm | | |
Help me if you can, I'm feeling down,
    |**G** | | | |
And I do appreciate you being 'round.
E | |
Help me get my feet back on the ground.
    |**A** | |**F♯m**
Won't you please, please help me?
    | |**A** | ‖
Help me, help me, ooh, mm.

Here Comes the Sun

Words and Music by
George Harrison

(Capo 7th fret)

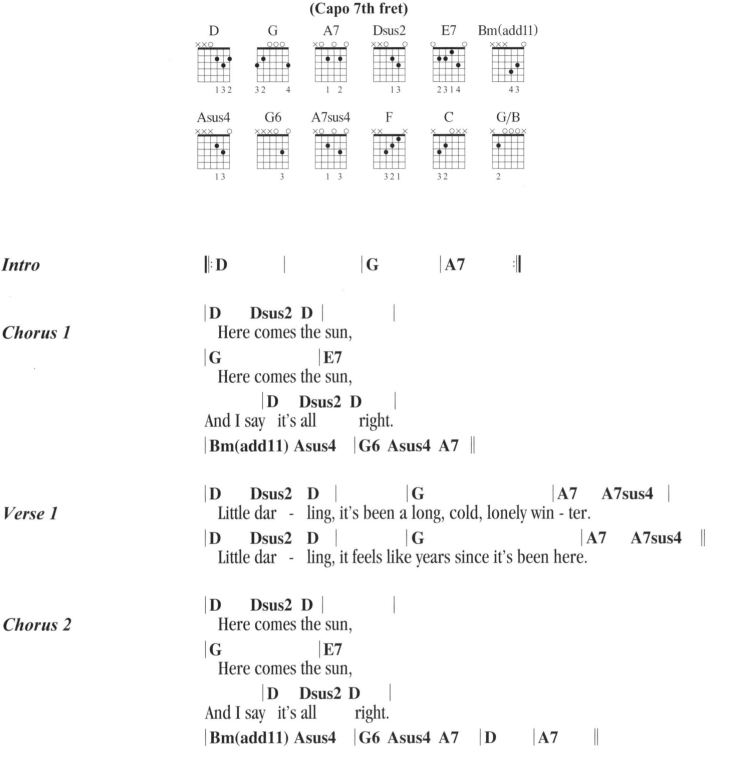

Intro

‖: D | | G | A7 :‖

Chorus 1

| D   Dsus2 D | |
Here comes the sun,

| G | E7
Here comes the sun,

| D   Dsus2 D |
And I say   it's all   right.

| Bm(add11) Asus4 | G6 Asus4 A7 ‖

Verse 1

| D   Dsus2 D | | G | A7   A7sus4 |
Little dar -   ling, it's been a long, cold, lonely win - ter.

| D   Dsus2 D | | G | A7   A7sus4 ‖
Little dar -   ling, it feels like years since it's been here.

Chorus 2

| D   Dsus2 D | |
Here comes the sun,

| G | E7
Here comes the sun,

| D   Dsus2 D |
And I say   it's all   right.

| Bm(add11) Asus4 | G6 Asus4 A7 | D | A7   ‖

Verse 2

```
|D    Dsus2  D  |              |G              |A7    A7sus4  |
 Little dar  -  ling, the smile's re - turning to their faces,
|D    Dsus2  D  |              |G              |A7    A7sus4  ||
 Little dar  -  ling, it seems like years since it's been here.
```

Chorus 3   *Repeat Chorus 2*

Bridge

```
|F    |C    |G/B  |G    |D    |A7    ||
|: F   |C    |G/B  |G    |D    |A7    :||  Play 5 times
  Sun,    sun,    sun,    here it comes.
|A7    |A7sus4  |A7    |A7sus4  A7    ||
```

Verse 3

```
|D    Dsus2  D  |              |G              |A7    A7sus4  |
 Little dar  -  ling, I feel that ice is slowly melt - ing.
|D    Dsus2  D  |              |G              |A7    A7sus4  ||
 Little dar  -  ling, it seems like years since it's been clear.
```

Chorus 4   *Repeat Chorus 1*

Chorus 5

```
|D    Dsus2  D  |              |
 Here comes the sun,
|G              |E7            |
 Here comes the sun,
|D              |
 It's alright.
|Bm(add11)  Asus4  |G6    Asus4  A7  |
|D              |
 It's all right.
|Bm(add11)  Asus4  |G6    Asus4  A7  |
|F    C  |G/B  G  |D            ||
```

Hey Jude

Words and Music by
John Lennon and Paul McCartney

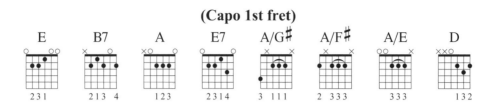

(Capo 1st fret)

Verse 1

    |**E** |**B7**
Hey Jude, don't make it bad.

    | |**E**
Take a sad song and make it better.

  |**A** |**E**
Re - member to let her into your heart,

        |**B7** |**E**
Then you can start to make it bet - ter.

Verse 2

    ‖**E** |**B7**
Hey Jude, don't be afraid.

    | |**E**
You were made to go out and get her.

  |**A** |**E**
The minute you let her under your skin,

        |**B7** |**E**   ‖
Then you be - gin to make it bet - ter.

Bridge 1

|E7 |A
And anytime you feel the pain,
   A/G♯ |A/F♯
Hey Jude, re - frain.
              |A/E |B7 |E
Don't car - ry the world   upon your shoul - ders.
|E7 |A
For well you know that it's a fool
      A/G♯ |A/F♯
Who plays it cool
          A/E |B7 |E
By mak - ing his world a little cold - er.
            |E7   B7 | |
Na, na, na, na, na, na, na, na, na.

Verse 3

      ‖E |B7
Hey Jude, don't let me down.
     | |E
You have found her, now go and get her.
  |A |E
Re - member to let her into your heart,
       |B7 |E   ‖
Then you can start to make it bet - ter.

Bridge 2

|E7 |A
    So let it out and let it in,

    A/G♯ |A/F♯
Hey Jude, be - gin,

             A/E |B7   E | |
You're wait - ing for some - one to per - form with.

|E7 |A
   And don't you know that it's just you,

    A/G♯ |A/F♯
Hey Jude, you'll do.

    A/E |B7 |E
The movement you need is on your should - er.

           |E7   B7 | |
Na, na, na, na, na, na, na, na, na. Yeah.

Verse 4

    ‖E |B7
Hey Jude, don't make it bad.

    | |E
Take a sad song and make it better.

   |A |E
Re - member to let her under your skin,

       |B7 |E
Then you be - gin to make it bet - ter,

           | ‖
Better, better, better, better, better, oh.

Outro

‖:E |D |
  Na,   na, na, na, na, na, na,

|A |E   :‖
  Na, na, na, na.   Hey Jude.   ***Repeat and fade***

Let It Be

Words and Music by
John Lennon and Paul McCartney

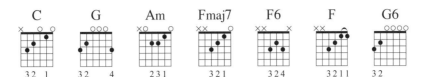

Intro
|C   G |Am   Fmaj7   F6 |C   G |F   C

Verse 1
||C   G |
When I find myself in times of trouble
|Am   Fmaj7   F6 |
 Mother Mary comes to me
|C   G
 Speaking words of wis - dom,
    |F   C
Let it be.

    | G
And in my hour of dark - ness
    |Am   Fmaj7   F6 |
She is standing right in front of me
|C   G
 Speaking words of wisdom,
    |F   C
Let it be.

Chorus 1
    ||Am   G6
Let it be, ___ let it be,
         |Fmaj7   C |
Ah, let it be, ___ let it be.
| G
Whisper words of wisdom,
    |F   C
Let it be.

Verse 2

```
                   ‖ C                  G                    |
                   And when the broken heart - ed people
                   | Am              Fmaj7    F6   |
                    Living in the world __ agree,
                   | C                G
                    There will be an an - swer,
                          | F     C
                   Let it be.
                        |                        G                    |
                   For though they may be part - ed there is
                   | Am              Fmaj7        F6   |
                    Still a chance that they __ will see
                   | C                G
                    There will be an an - swer,
                          | F     C
                   Let it be.
```

Chorus 2

```
                          ‖ Am          G6
                   Let it be, __ let it be,
                           | Fmaj7          C    |
                   Ah, let it be, __ let it be.
                   |                        G
                    Yeah, there will be an an - swer,
                          | F     C
                   Let it be.
```

Chorus 3   *Repeat Chorus 1*

Interlude | F   C | G F C | F   C | G F C ‖

Guitar Solo | C   G | Am Fmaj7 F6 | C   G | F   C |
                  | G | Am Fmaj7 F6 | C   G | F   C

Chorus 4   *Repeat Chorus 1*

Verse 3

‖C   G

And when the night is cloud - y

      |Am   Fmaj7   F6 |

There is still a light that shines on me;

|C   G

 Shine until tomor - row,

    |F   C

Let it be.

| G |

I wake up to the sound __ of music;

|Am   Fmaj7   F6 |

 Mother Mary comes __ to me,

|C   G

 Speaking words of wisdom,

    |F   C

Let it be.

Chorus 5

        ‖Am   G6

Let it be, __ let it be,

      |Fmaj7   C

Ah, let it be, __ let it be.

| G

Yeah, there will be an an - swer,

   |F   C

Let it be.

      |Am   G6

Let it be, __ let it be,

      |Fmaj7   C |

Ah, let it be, __ let it be.

| G

Whisper words of wisdom,

   |F   C |F   C |G   F   C ‖

Let it be.

I Saw Her Standing There

Words and Music by
John Lennon and Paul McCartney

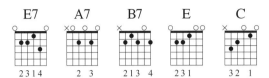

Intro

|N.C. |E7 | | | |
One, two, three, four!

Verse 1

|E7 || |
Well, she was just seventeen,
| |A7 |E7
You know what I mean,
| | |B7 |
And the way she looked was way beyond com - pare.
| |E |E7 |A7 |C
So how could I dance with anoth - er, woo,
|E7 |B7 |E7 |
When I saw her standing there?

Verse 2

| ||E7 |
Well, she looked at me,
| |A7 |E7
And I, I could see
| | |B7 | |
That be - fore too long I'd fall in love with her.
|E |E7 |A7 |C
She wouldn't dance with anoth - er, woo,
|E7 |B7 |E7 |
When I saw her standing there.

Bridge

   | ‖**A7** |

Well, my heart went boom

   | | |

When I crossed that room

   | | | |**B7** | |**A7** |

And I held her hand   in   mine.

Verse 3

   | ‖**E7** |

Oh, we danced   through the night,

   | |**A7** |**E7**

And we held each other tight,

    | | |**B7** |

And be‑fore too long I fell in love with her.

   | |**E** |**E7** |**A7** |**C**

Now I'll never dance   with anoth‑er,   woo,

   |**E7** |**B7** |**E7** | ‖

Since I saw her   standing there.

Interlude

|**E7** | | | | | |**B7** | |

|**E7** | |**A7** | |**E7** |**B7** |**E7**   ‖

Repeat Bridge

Repeat Verse 3

Outro

|**E7** | |**B7** |**E7** |

Oh, since I saw her   standing there.

| |**E7** |**B7** |**A7** |**E7** | ‖

Yeah, well, since I saw her   standing there.

I Want to Hold Your Hand

Words and Music by
John Lennon and Paul McCartney

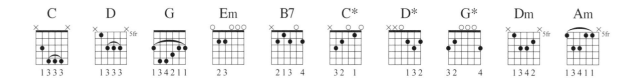

Intro　　　　　　| 　 C D | 　 C D | 　 C D | 　　　　|

Verse 1

| 　 ‖G 　 |D 　　|
Oh yeah, I tell you something,
|Em 　　　　　|B7
I think you'll under - stand.
　 |G 　 |D 　　　|
When I say that something,
|Em 　　　　　|B7 　　 ‖
I wanna hold your hand.

Chorus 1

|C* 　　 D* 　 |G* Em 　|
I wanna hold your hand,
|C* 　　 D* 　 |G* 　　　|
I wanna hold your hand.

Verse 2

　‖G 　　 |D 　　|
Oh please, say to me
|Em 　　　　|B7
You'll let me be your man.
　 |G 　 |D 　|
And please say to me
|Em 　　　　|B7 　　 ‖
You'll let me hold your hand.

Chorus 2

|C* 　　　 D* 　 |G* Em 　|
Now let me hold your hand,
|C* 　 D* 　|G* 　　　 ‖
I wanna hold your hand.

Bridge 1

```
|Dm          |G
  And when I touch you
      |C        |Am         |
I feel happy in - side.
|Dm          |G
  It's such a feeling
         |C          |D
That my love I can't hide,
C      |D    C    |D          |
I can't hide, I can't hide.
```

Verse 3

```
       ‖G          |D          |
Yeah, you got that something,
|Em                 |B7
  I think you'll under - stand.
   |G         |D          |
When I say that something,
|Em                 |B7         ‖
  I wanna hold your hand.
```

Chorus 3   *Repeat Chorus 1*

Bridge 2   *Repeat Bridge 1*

Verse 4

```
       ‖G          |D          |
Yeah, you got that something,
|Em                 |B7
  I think you'll under - stand.
   |G         |D          |
When I feel that something,
|Em                 |B7         ‖
  I wanna hold your hand.
```

Chorus 4

```
|C*       D*      |G*  Em   |
  I wanna hold your hand.
|C*       D*      |B7       |
  I wanna hold your hand.
|C*       D*      |C*  |G*   ‖
  I wanna hold your hand.
```

In My Life

Words and Music by
John Lennon and Paul McCartney

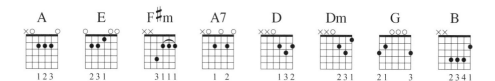

Intro |A |E |A |E

                                              ‖A   E |F#m   A7
Verse 1   There are places I re - member
                             |D   Dm |A
                     All my life, _____ though some have changed.
                             | E |F#m   A7
                     Some for - ever, not for better,
                             |D   Dm |A
                     Some have gone, _____ and some remain.

                             ‖F#m |D
Chorus 1   All these places had their moments,
                             |G |A
                     With lovers and friends I still can recall,
                             |F#m |B
                     Some are dead and some are living,
                             |Dm |A | E |
                     In my life, I've loved them all.

Verse 2

```
        ‖A        E        |F♯m      A7
But of all these friends and lovers,
              |D  Dm         |A
There is no  one com - pares with you.
              |          E        |F♯m      A7
And these memories lose their meaning
              |D        Dm      |A
When I think of love as something new.
```

Chorus 2

```
              ‖F♯m                    |D
Though I know I'll never lose af - fection
      |G                      |A
For people and things that went before,
  |F♯m                              |B
I know I'll often stop and think a - bout them.
  |Dm        |A                  ‖
In my life, I love you more.
```

Solo

```
|A      E    |F♯m A7  |D    Dm  |A              |
|        E    |F♯m A7  |D    Dm  |A
```

Chorus 3

```
              ‖F♯m                    |D
Though I know I'll never lose af - fection
      |G                      |A
For people and things that went before,
  |F♯m                              |B
I know I'll often stop and think a - bout them.
  |Dm        |A              |        E |
In my life, I love you more.
  |Dm                |A      E |      |A        ‖
In my life, I love you more.
```

The Long and Winding Road

Words and Music by
John Lennon and Paul McCartney

(Capo 1st fret)

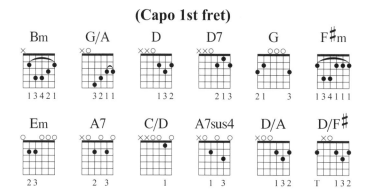

Verse 1

```
| Bm                   |G/A
The long and winding road
 |D    D7       |G       |
That leads to your door
 |       F#m        |Bm       |
   Will never disap - pear.
|Em            A7     |C/D  D |
   I've seen that road be - fore.
|G  F#m    |Bm              |
   It always leads me here,
|Em         A7 A7sus4|D
   Lead me to   your   door.
```

Verse 2

```
  || Bm                 |G/A
The wild and windy night
           |D   D7      |G      |
That the rain washed a - way,
 |       F#m |Bm          |
   Has left a   pool of tears
|Em     A7    |C/D  D |
   Crying for the day.
|G   F#m             |Bm           |
   Why leave me stand - ing here?
|Em     A7    A7sus4 |D           ||
   Let me know the      way.
```

Bridge

  | D/A   G
  Many times I've been alone,
   | D/F♯   Em A7 |
  And many times I've cried.
  | D/A   G
  Anyway, you'll never know
   | D/F♯   Em A7
  The many ways I've tried.

Verse 3

   ‖ Bm | G/A
  And still they lead me back
     | D D7 | G |
  To the long, winding road.
  | F♯m | Bm |
  You left me stand - ing here
  | Em A7 | C/D D |
  A long, long time ago.
  | G F♯m | Bm |
  Don't leave me wait - ing here,
  | Em A7 A7sus4 | D   ‖
  Lead me to your door.

Interlude

  ‖: D/A G | D/F♯ Em A7 :‖

Verse 4

   | Bm | G/A
  But still they lead me back
     | D D7 | G |
  To the long, winding road.
  | F♯m | Bm |
  You left me standing here
  | Em A7 | C/D D |
  A long, long time ago.
  | G F♯m | Bm |
  Don't keep me wait - ing here,
  | Em A7 | D |
  Lead me to your ___ door.
  | G/A   D | | ‖
  Yeah, yeah, yeah, yeah.

Ob-La-Di, Ob-La-Da

Words and Music by
John Lennon and Paul McCartney

(Capo 1st fret)

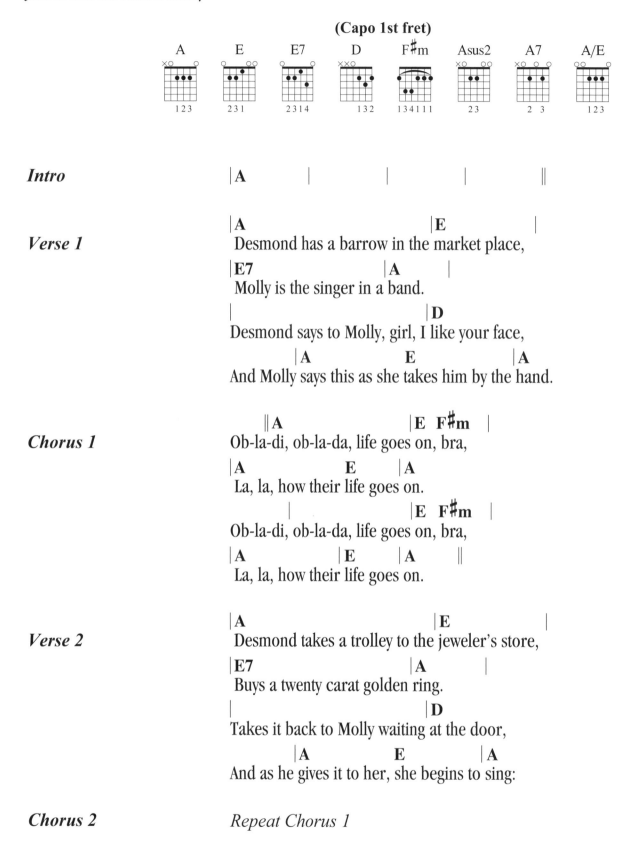

Intro

|A | | | ||

Verse 1

|A |E |
 Desmond has a barrow in the market place,

|E7 |A |
 Molly is the singer in a band.

| |D
 Desmond says to Molly, girl, I like your face,

      |A   E |A
 And Molly says this as she takes him by the hand.

Chorus 1

     ‖A |E F#m |
 Ob-la-di, ob-la-da, life goes on, bra,

|A   E |A
 La, la, how their life goes on.

      | |E F#m |
 Ob-la-di, ob-la-da, life goes on, bra,

|A |E |A   ‖
 La, la, how their life goes on.

Verse 2

|A |E |
 Desmond takes a trolley to the jeweler's store,

|E7 |A |
 Buys a twenty carat golden ring.

| |D
 Takes it back to Molly waiting at the door,

      |A   E |A
 And as he gives it to her, she begins to sing:

Chorus 2   *Repeat Chorus 1*

Bridge 1

|D
  In a couple of years,

      | |A Asus2 |A A7 |
They have built a home sweet home.

|D |
  With a couple of kids running in the yard

  |A/E |E ||
Of Desmond and Molly Jones.

Verse 3

|A |E |
 Happy ever after in the market place,

|E7 |A |
 Desmond lets the children lend a hand.

| |D
Molly stays at home and does her pretty face,

      |A   E |A
And in the evening she still sings it with the band.

Chorus 3   *Repeat Chorus 1*

Bridge 2   *Repeat Bridge 1*

Verse 4

|A |E |
 Happy ever after in the market place,

|E7 |A |
 Molly lets the children lend a hand.

| |D
Desmond stays at home and does his pretty face,

      |A   E |A
And in the evening she's a singer with the band.

Chorus 4

      ||A |E F#m |
Ob-la-di, ob-la-da, life goes on, bra,

|A   E |A
 La, la, how their life goes on.

        | |E F#m |
Ob-la-di, ob-la-da, life goes on, bra,

|A |E |F#m
 La, la, how their life goes on.

        |
And if you want some fun,

  |E   A ||
Take ob-la-di-bla-da.

Something

Words and Music by
George Harrison

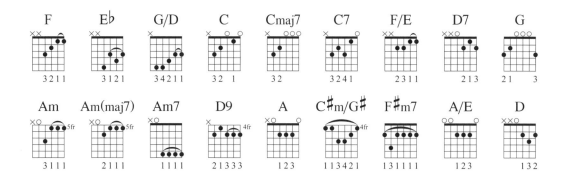

Intro

|**F**   **E♭**   **G/D** ||

Verse 1

|**C** |**Cmaj7** |
Something in the way she moves

|**C7** |**F**   **F/E** |
 Attracts me like no other lover.

|**D7** |**G** |
Something in the way she woos me.

|**Am**   **Am(maj7)**
I don't want to leave her now,

    |**Am7**   **D9** |**F** **E♭** **G/D** ||
You know I believe, and how.

Verse 2

|**C** |**Cmaj7** |
Somewhere in her smile she knows

|**C7** |**F**   **F/E** |
 That I don't need no other lover.

|**D7** |**G** |
Something in her style that shows me.

|**Am**   **Am(maj7)**
I don't want to leave her now,

    |**Am7**   **D9** |
You know I believe, and how.

|**F** **E♭** **G/D** |**A** ||

Bridge

```
|A              C♯m/G♯        |F♯m7   A/E
  You're asking me will my love grow,
       |D      G    |A          |
I don't know, I don't know.
|              C♯m/G♯            |F♯m7     A/E
  You stick around now, it may show,
       |D      G    |C           ‖
I don't know, I don't know.
```

Interlude

```
|C        |Cmaj7  |C7      |F  F/E |D7      |G         |
|Am  Am(maj7)  |Am7   D9       |F    E♭  G/D  ‖
```

Verse 3

```
|C                              |Cmaj7      |
 Something in the way she knows,
|C7                    |F              F/E  |
   And all I have to do is think of her.
|D7                      |G
 Something in the things she shows me.
 |Am                        Am(maj7)
I don't want to leave her now,
      |Am7                  D9      ‖
You know I believe, and how.
```

Outro

```
|F  E♭  G/D |A         |F  E♭  G/D |C            ‖
```

Yesterday

Words and Music by
John Lennon and Paul McCartney

(Tune down 1 step)

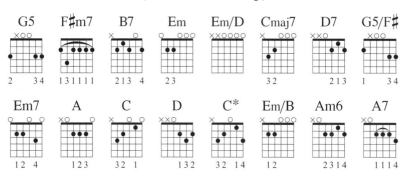

Intro |G5 | ‖

Verse 1
|G5 |
Yesterday
|F♯m7   B7 |Em   Em/D |
   All my troubles seemed so far away.
|Cmaj7   D7 |G5
   Now it looks as though they're here to stay.
G5/F♯|Em7   A |C   G5   ‖
Oh,   I believe   in yes - terday.

Verse 2
|G5 |
Suddenly
|F♯m7   B7 |Em   Em/D |
   I'm not half the man I used to be.
|Cmaj7   D7 |G5
   There's a shadow hanging over me.
G5/F♯|Em7   A |C   G5   ‖
Oh,   yesterday   came sud - denly.

Bridge

|F♯m7 B7 |Em D C*
Why she had to go
Em/B |Am6   D7 |G5 |
I   don't know, she wouldn't say.
|F♯m7 B7 |Em   D   C*
I   said some - thing wrong,
 Em/B |Am6   D7 |G5 ||
Now I long for yester - day.

Verse 3

|G5 |
Yesterday
|F♯m7   B7 |Em   Em/D|
   Love was such an easy game to play.
|Cmaj7   D7 |G5
   Now I need a place to hide away.
G5/F♯ |Em7   A |C G5 ||
Oh,   I believe in yes - terday.

Repeat Bridge

Repeat Verse 3

|G5   A7 |C* G5 ||
Hmm._____

She Loves You

Words and Music by
John Lennon and Paul McCartney

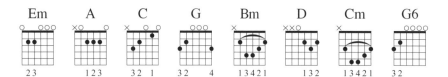

Chorus 1

|Em |
She loves you, yeah,   yeah, yeah.
|A |
She loves you, yeah,   yeah, yeah.
|C | |G |
She loves you, yeah,   yeah, yeah,   yeah.

Verse 1

| ‖G |Em
    You think you lost your love?
|Bm |D
Well, I saw her yester - day.
|G |Em
It's you she's thinking of
|Bm |D
And she told me what to say:
|G
She says she loves you
| |Em |
And you know that can't be bad.
|Cm
Yes, she loves you
| |D |
And you know you should be glad.

Verse 2

  | ‖**G** |**Em**

She said you hurt her so,

 |**Bm** |**D**

She almost lost her mind.

 |**G** |**Em**

But now she said she knows

   |**Bm** |**D**

You're not the hurting kind.

        |**G**

She says she loves you

    | |**Em** |

And you know that can't be bad.

  |**Cm**

Yes, she loves you

  | |**D** |

And you know you should be glad,   ooh!

Chorus 2

 | ‖**Em** |

She loves you, yeah, yeah, yeah.

 |**A** |

She loves you, yeah, yeah, yeah.

    |**Cm**

And with a love like that

 |**D** |**G** |

You know you should be glad.

Verse 3

```
|        ||G                        |Em
      You know it's up to you;
 |Bm            |D                |
I think it's only fair.
|G                            |Em
Pride can hurt you too;
  |Bm          |D
A - pologize to her
                       |G
Because she loves you
           |                    |Em                |
And you know that can't be bad.
|           |Cm
   Yes, she loves you
           |                    |D              |
And you know you should be glad,          ooh!
```

Chorus 3

```
     |      ||Em              |
      She loves you, yeah,   yeah, yeah.
    |A              |
She loves you, yeah,   yeah, yeah.
            |Cm
And with a love like that
   |D                      |G            |Em
You know you should be glad.
      |Cm
With a love like that
   |D                      |G            |Em
You know you should be glad.
      |Cm
With a love like that,
   |D                |G          |          |
You know you should be glad.
|Em           |            |
     Yeah,   yeah, yeah.
|C          |          |G6           ||
     Yeah,   yeah,  yeah,  yeah!
```

STRUM & SING

Lyrics, chord symbols, and guitar chord diagrams for your favorite songs.

GUITAR

ACOUSTIC CLASSICS
00191891......$12.99

ADELE
00159855......$12.99

SARA BAREILLES
00102354......$12.99

THE BEATLES
00172234......$16.99

BLUES
00159335......$12.99

ZAC BROWN BAND
02501620......$14.99

COLBIE CAILLAT
02501725......$14.99

CAMPFIRE FOLK SONGS
02500686......$14.99

CHART HITS OF 2014-2015
00142554......$12.99

CHART HITS OF 2015-2016
00156248......$12.99

BEST OF KENNY CHESNEY
00142457......$14.99

CHRISTMAS SONGS
00171332......$14.99

KELLY CLARKSON
00146384......$14.99

LEONARD COHEN
00265489......$12.99

JOHN DENVER COLLECTION
02500632......$12.99

EAGLES
00157994......$12.99

EASY ACOUSTIC SONGS
00125478......$14.99

THE 5 CHORD SONGBOOK
02501718......$12.99

FOLK SONGS
02501482......$10.99

FOLK/ROCK FAVORITES
02501669......$12.99

FOUR CHORD SONGS
00249581......$14.99

THE 4 CHORD SONGBOOK
02501533......$12.99

THE 4-CHORD COUNTRY SONGBOOK
00114936......$15.99

THE GREATEST SHOWMAN
00278383......$14.99

HAMILTON
00217116......$14.99

HITS OF THE '70S
02500871......$9.99

JACK JOHNSON
02500858......$16.99

ROBERT JOHNSON
00191890......$12.99

CAROLE KING
00115243......$10.99

BEST OF GORDON LIGHTFOOT
00139393......$14.99

DAVE MATTHEWS BAND
02501078......$10.95

JOHN MAYER
02501636......$10.99

INGRID MICHAELSON
02501634......$10.99

THE MOST REQUESTED SONGS
02501748......$14.99

JASON MRAZ
02501452......$14.99

PRAISE & WORSHIP
00152381......$12.99

ELVIS PRESLEY
00198890......$12.99

QUEEN
00218578......$12.99

ROCK AROUND THE CLOCK
00103625......$12.99

ROCK BALLADS
02500872......$9.95

ED SHEERAN
00152016......$14.99

THE 6 CHORD SONGBOOK
02502277......$12.99

CAT STEVENS
00116827......$14.99

TAYLOR SWIFT
00159856......$12.99

THE 3 CHORD SONGBOOK
00211634......$10.99

TODAY'S HITS
00119301......$12.99

TOP CHRISTIAN HITS
00156331......$12.99

TOP HITS OF 2016
00194288......$12.99

KEITH URBAN
00118558......$14.99

THE WHO
00103667......$12.99

NEIL YOUNG – GREATEST HITS
00138270......$14.99

UKULELE

THE BEATLES
00233899......$16.99

COLBIE CAILLAT
02501731......$10.99

JOHN DENVER
02501694......$10.99

FOLK ROCK FAVORITES FOR UKULELE
00114600......$12.99

THE 4-CHORD UKULELE SONGBOOK
00114331......$14.99

JACK JOHNSON
02501702......$19.99

JOHN MAYER
02501706......$10.99

INGRID MICHAELSON
02501741......$12.99

THE MOST REQUESTED SONGS
02501453......$14.99

JASON MRAZ
02501753......$14.99

SING-ALONG SONGS
02501710......$15.99

HAL•LEONARD®

www.halleonard.com
Visit our website to see full song lists.

Prices, content, and availability subject to change without notice.

EASY GUITAR WITH NOTES & TAB

This series features simplified arrangements with notes, tab, chord charts, and strum and pick patterns.

MIXED FOLIOS

00702287	Acoustic	$16.99
00702002	Acoustic Rock Hits for Easy Guitar	$14.99
00702166	All-Time Best Guitar Collection	$19.99
00702232	Best Acoustic Songs for Easy Guitar	$14.99
00119835	Best Children's Songs	$16.99
00702233	Best Hard Rock Songs	$14.99
00703055	The Big Book of Nursery Rhymes & Children's Songs	$16.99
00322179	The Big Easy Book of Classic Rock Guitar	$24.95
00698978	Big Christmas Collection	$17.99
00702394	Bluegrass Songs for Easy Guitar	$12.99
00289632	Bohemian Rhapsody	$17.99
00703387	Celtic Classics	$14.99
00224808	Chart Hits of 2016-2017	$14.99
00267383	Chart Hits of 2017-2018	$14.99
00702149	Children's Christian Songbook	$9.99
00702028	Christmas Classics	$8.99
00101779	Christmas Guitar	$14.99
00702185	Christmas Hits	$10.99
00702141	Classic Rock	$8.95
00159642	Classical Melodies	$12.99
00253933	Disney/Pixar's Coco	$16.99
00702203	CMT's 100 Greatest Country Songs	$29.99

00702283	The Contemporary Christian Collection	$16.99
00196954	Contemporary Disney	$16.99
00702239	Country Classics for Easy Guitar	$22.99
00702257	Easy Acoustic Guitar Songs	$14.99
00702280	Easy Guitar Tab White Pages	$29.99
00702041	Favorite Hymns for Easy Guitar	$10.99
00222701	Folk Pop Songs	$14.99
00140841	4-Chord Hymns for Guitar	$9.99
00702281	4 Chord Rock	$10.99
00126894	Frozen	$14.99
00702286	Glee	$16.99
00699374	Gospel Favorites	$16.99
00702160	The Great American Country Songbook	$16.99
00702050	Great Classical Themes for Easy Guitar	$8.99
00702116	Greatest Hymns for Guitar	$10.99
00275088	The Greatest Showman	$17.99
00148030	Halloween Guitar Songs	$14.99
00702273	Irish Songs	$12.99
00192503	Jazz Classics for Easy Guitar	$14.99
00702275	Jazz Favorites for Easy Guitar	$15.99
00702274	Jazz Standards for Easy Guitar	$15.99
00702162	Jumbo Easy Guitar Songbook	$19.99
00232285	La La Land	$16.99
00702258	Legends of Rock	$14.99
00702189	MTV's 100 Greatest Pop Songs	$24.95

00702272	1950s Rock	$15.99
00702271	1960s Rock	$15.99
00702270	1970s Rock	$15.99
00702269	1980s Rock	$15.99
00702268	1990s Rock	$15.99
00109725	Once	$14.99
00702187	Selections from O Brother Where Art Thou?	$15.99
00702178	100 Songs for Kids	$14.99
00702515	Pirates of the Caribbean	$14.99
00702125	Praise and Worship for Guitar	$10.99
00287930	Songs from A Star Is Born, The Greatest Showman, La La Land, and More Movie Musicals	$16.99
00702285	Southern Rock Hits	$12.99
00156420	Star Wars Music	$14.99
00121535	30 Easy Celtic Guitar Solos	$15.99
00702220	Today's Country Hits	$12.99
00121900	Today's Women of Pop & Rock	$14.99
00244654	Top Hits of 2017	$14.99
00283786	Top Hits of 2018	$14.99
00702294	Top Worship Hits	$15.99
00702255	VH1's 100 Greatest Hard Rock Songs	$27.99
00702175	VH1's 100 Greatest Songs of Rock and Roll	$24.99
00702253	Wicked	$12.99

ARTIST COLLECTIONS

00702267	AC/DC for Easy Guitar	$15.99
00702598	Adele for Easy Guitar	$15.99
00156221	Adele – 25	$16.99
00702040	Best of the Allman Brothers	$15.99
00702865	J.S. Bach for Easy Guitar	$14.99
00702169	Best of The Beach Boys	$12.99
00702292	The Beatles — 1	$19.99
00125796	Best of Chuck Berry	$15.99
00702201	The Essential Black Sabbath	$12.95
02501615	Zac Brown Band — The Foundation	$16.99
02501621	Zac Brown Band — You Get What You Give	$16.99
00702043	Best of Johnny Cash	$16.99
00702090	Eric Clapton's Best	$12.99
00702086	Eric Clapton — from the Album Unplugged	$14.99
00702202	The Essential Eric Clapton	$14.99
00702250	blink-182 — Greatest Hits	$15.99
00702053	Best of Patsy Cline	$15.99
00222697	Very Best of Coldplay – 2nd Edition	$14.99
00702229	The Very Best of Creedence Clearwater Revival	$15.99
00702145	Best of Jim Croce	$15.99
00702278	Crosby, Stills & Nash	$12.99
14042809	Bob Dylan	$14.99
00702276	Fleetwood Mac — Easy Guitar Collection	$14.99
00139462	The Very Best of Grateful Dead	$15.99
00702136	Best of Merle Haggard	$12.99
00702227	Jimi Hendrix — Smash Hits	$16.99
00702288	Best of Hillsong United	$12.99
00702236	Best of Antonio Carlos Jobim	$14.99
00702245	Elton John — Greatest Hits 1970–2002	$17.99

00129855	Jack Johnson	$16.99
00702204	Robert Johnson	$10.99
00702234	Selections from Toby Keith — 35 Biggest Hits	$12.95
00702003	Kiss	$12.99
00702216	Lynyrd Skynyrd	$15.99
00702182	The Essential Bob Marley	$14.94
00146081	Maroon 5	$14.99
00121925	Bruno Mars – Unorthodox Jukebox	$12.99
00702248	Paul McCartney — All the Best	$14.99
00702129	Songs of Sarah McLachlan	$12.95
00125484	The Best of MercyMe	$12.99
02501316	Metallica — Death Magnetic	$19.99
00702209	Steve Miller Band — Young Hearts (Greatest Hits)	$12.95
00124167	Jason Mraz	$15.99
00702096	Best of Nirvana	$15.99
00702211	The Offspring — Greatest Hits	$12.95
00138026	One Direction	$14.99
00702030	Best of Roy Orbison	$15.99
00702144	Best of Ozzy Osbourne	$14.99
00702279	Tom Petty	$12.99
00102911	Pink Floyd	$16.99
00702139	Elvis Country Favorites	$15.99
00702293	The Very Best of Prince	$15.99
00699415	Best of Queen for Guitar	$15.99
00109279	Best of R.E.M.	$14.99
00702208	Red Hot Chili Peppers — Greatest Hits	$15.99
00198960	The Rolling Stones	$16.99
00174793	The Very Best of Santana	$14.99
00702196	Best of Bob Seger	$12.95
00146046	Ed Sheeran	$14.99
00702252	Frank Sinatra — Nothing But the Best	$12.99

00702010	Best of Rod Stewart	$16.99
00702049	Best of George Strait	$14.99
00702259	Taylor Swift for Easy Guitar	$15.99
00254499	Taylor Swift – Easy Guitar Anthology	$19.99
00702260	Taylor Swift — Fearless	$14.99
00139727	Taylor Swift — 1989	$17.99
00115960	Taylor Swift — Red	$16.99
00253667	Taylor Swift — Reputation	$17.99
00702290	Taylor Swift — Speak Now	$15.99
00232849	Chris Tomlin Collection – 2nd Edition	$14.99
00702226	Chris Tomlin — See the Morning	$12.95
00148643	Train	$14.99
00702427	U2 — 18 Singles	$16.99
00702108	Best of Stevie Ray Vaughan	$16.99
00279005	The Who	$14.99
00702123	Best of Hank Williams	$14.99
00194548	Best of John Williams	$14.99
00702111	Stevie Wonder — Guitar Collection	$9.99
00702228	Neil Young — Greatest Hits	$15.99
00119133	Neil Young — Harvest	$14.99
00702188	Essential ZZ Top	$14.99

Prices, contents and availability
subject to change without notice.

Visit Hal Leonard online at **halleonard.com**

0319
306